THE HUMAN BODY

THE DIGESTIVE SYSTEM

By John M. Shea, MD

Gareth Stevens
Publishing

Please visit our website, www.garethstevens.com. For a free color catalog of all our high-quality books, call toll free 1-800-542-2595 or fax 1-877-542-2596.

Library of Congress Cataloging-in-Publication Data

Shea, John M.
The digestive system / John M. Shea.
    p. cm. — (The human body)
Includes index.
ISBN 978-1-4339-6582-1 (pbk.)
ISBN 978-1-4339-6583-8 (6-pack)
ISBN 978-1-4339-6624-8 (library binding)
1. Gastrointestinal system—Juvenile literature. I. Title.
QP145.S44 2012
612.3'2—dc23

                              2011023268

First Edition

Published in 2012 by
Gareth Stevens Publishing
111 East 14th Street, Suite 349
New York, NY 10003

Copyright © 2012 Gareth Stevens Publishing

Designer: Daniel Hosek
Editor: Greg Roza

Photo credits: Cover, pp. 1, 13 (liver), 23 (all images), 25 Thinkstock.com; all backgrounds, pp. 7, 9, 11 (all images), 13 (main image, villi), 28–29 Shutterstock.com; pp. 5, 15 (gallstones), 17 (main) Dorling Kindersley/Getty Images; p. 15 (main image) MedicalRF.com/ Getty Images; p. 17 (colon bacteria) Ingram Publishing/The Agency Collection/Getty Images; pp. 19, 21 iStockphoto.com; p. 27 (main) Thinkstock/Comstock Images/Getty Images.

Printed in the United States of America

CPSIA compliance information: Batch #CW12GS: For further information contact Gareth Stevens, New York, New York at 1-800-542-2595.

Contents

Words in the glossary appear in **bold** type
the first time they are used in the text.

Why Do We Eat?

All living things need nutrients to survive. Nutrients are chemicals found in food that provide energy and materials the body needs to grow. Some living things, such as plants, make their own food from sunlight. Other creatures, such as extremely small **bacteria**, only need a tiny amount of nutrients to grow.

The human body, however, is very complex. It needs a lot of nutrients to maintain it. The food we eat—whether it's an apple, pizza, cake, or a glass of milk—contains nutrients our body needs. But first, our bodies must break these foods down into very small pieces so we can use the nutrients in them. The process of breaking down food into basic nutrients is called digestion.

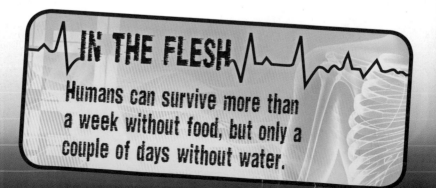

IN THE FLESH

Humans can survive more than a week without food, but only a couple of days without water.

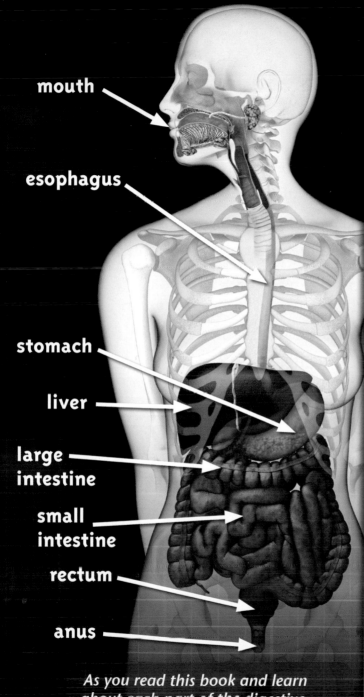

mouth

esophagus

stomach

liver

large intestine

small intestine

rectum

anus

It's best to think of the digestive system as one continuous tract, or tube. It starts with the mouth, where we put food in, and ends with the anus, where undigested waste leaves our bodies. Every part of the digestive system has a specific job to help us get the most nutrients from our food. Most jobs involve breaking down food and moving nutrients from the digestive tract to the bloodstream.

As you read this book and learn about each part of the digestive system, look back to this picture to see where in the body you are and predict where we'll go next.

Food for Life

Foods contain different nutrients, each with a special role to play in our health. Carbohydrates, which include sugars and **starches**, are the body's main source of energy. Proteins—which are made up of smaller chemicals called amino acids—are the basic building blocks for the human body. Lipids, sometimes known as fats, are made from smaller chemicals called fatty acids. They're important for both growth and energy.

Water is an extremely important nutrient. More that half our body is made of water, and we need to drink enough every day to help keep our body well **hydrated**. Fiber is a unique nutrient. Our bodies don't digest and absorb fiber for growth and health. Instead, undigested fiber helps push food forward through the digestive tract.

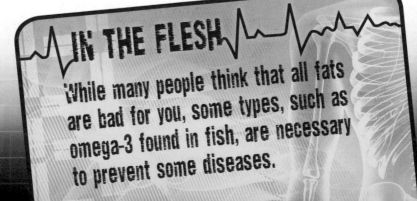

IN THE FLESH

While many people think that all fats are bad for you, some types, such as omega-3 found in fish, are necessary to prevent some diseases.

No single food has all the nutrients we need. We must eat a wide variety of foods to make sure we get all the nutrients necessary to stay healthy and grow.

VITAMINS AND MINERALS

While we only need tiny amounts of vitamins and minerals each day, each plays a very special role in our health. For example, vitamin A is used by the eyes to help with vision. Vitamin C is used by the **immune system** to help fight off illnesses and to heal cuts. Minerals are nutrients that plants take in from the soil. The human body needs minerals, such as calcium and zinc, to maintain chemical reactions.

The Starting Line

The first step in transforming food into nutrients begins in the mouth. Teeth bite and grind food into smaller, softer pieces. The mouth produces saliva, or spit, which makes food easier to chew and swallow. Saliva also contains chemicals known as **enzymes**. Enzymes begin to break food down into nutrients small enough for the body to absorb.

Once the food is small and soft enough, it's ready to be swallowed. The tongue pushes the food toward the back of the throat and down a muscular tube, called the esophagus, that connects the mouth to the stomach. When the muscles of the esophagus become stretched with food, they squeeze and push the food down in a process called peristalsis.

IN THE FLESH

Children have 20 teeth, and adults have 32. Most adults get their third set of molars—known as "wisdom teeth"—around age 20.

FOOD AND THE SENSES

The human tongue is covered with tiny bumps called "taste buds" that recognize foods that taste sweet, salty, sour, and bitter. Some people even have a fifth kind of taste bud, called "umami," that can recognize savory, meaty flavors. While the tongue can recognize five tastes, the nose can recognize over 10,000 different smells! Most of what we think of as taste is really smell, which explains why food tastes so bland when we have a cold.

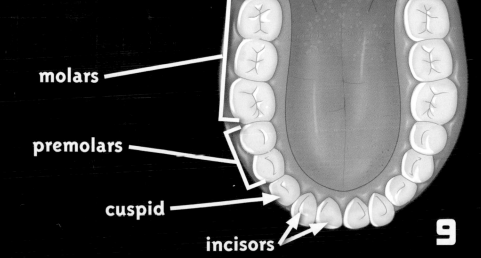

Cuspids help the jaw grab onto food. Incisors cut food into smaller pieces. Premolars and molars grind food into smaller, softer pieces.

molars

premolars

cuspid

incisors

The Digestive Warehouse

From the esophagus, food empties into the stomach. This is a muscular sac about the size of your fist, but it can expand to hold a large meal. The stomach contains an extremely strong acid that helps **dissolve** food while also killing many types of bacteria. The stomach produces an enzyme called pepsin that breaks down proteins into amino acids.

The stomach can hold food from your last meal for hours. It slowly releases partially digested food into the next part of the digestive system—the small intestine—a little at a time. Any food that's too big for the small intestine stays in the stomach longer, where the acid and pepsin continue to break it down further.

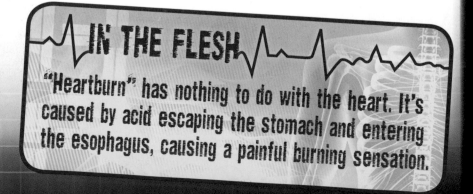

IN THE FLESH

"Heartburn" has nothing to do with the heart. It's caused by acid escaping the stomach and entering the esophagus, causing a painful burning sensation.

Even though many people call their abdomen, or belly, their "stomach," most of the abdomen is made up of the small and large intestines.

esophagus

stomach

to small intestine

ULCERS

ulcer →

Ulcers are small wounds in the stomach and small intestine walls that can be extremely painful. For many years, doctors thought ulcers were caused by stress and too much stomach acid. Recently, scientists have discovered that a bacterium called *Helicobacter pylori* is the most common cause of the wounds. Drugs that kill bacteria, called antibiotics, have helped cure many people of this painful condition.

11

The Small Intestine's Big Job

The small intestine is where most of the digestion and absorption of nutrients takes place. Food coming from the stomach mixes with enzymes and fluids coming from the pancreas. The fluids **neutralize** the stomach acids, while the enzymes finish breaking down the food into the basic building blocks of nutrition: amino acids, sugars, fatty acids, vitamins, and minerals.

On the inside wall of the small intestine are thousands of very tiny, finger-like folds called villi. The villi have special channels, or tunnels, that allow the nutrients to leave the small intestine and enter the bloodstream. When the food we ate exits the small intestine, there's nothing left but water, some minerals, and material we can't digest, such as fiber.

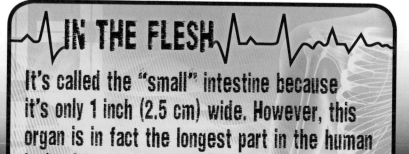

IN THE FLESH

It's called the "small" intestine because it's only 1 inch (2.5 cm) wide. However, this organ is in fact the longest part in the human body—it's over 20 feet (6 m) long!

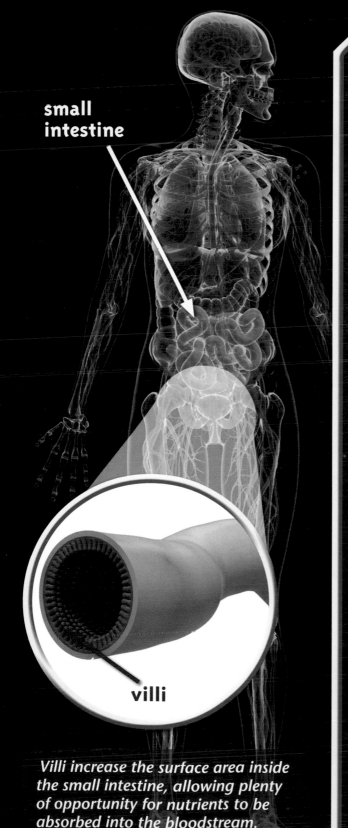

small
intestine

villi

*Villi increase the surface area inside
the small intestine, allowing plenty
of opportunity for nutrients to be
absorbed into the bloodstream.*

While it isn't
connected directly to
the digestive tract,
the liver plays an
important role in
digestion, too. When
nutrients are absorbed
into the blood by the
small intestine, they're
first carried to the
liver. The liver stores
some of these nutrients
for future use. It also
protects the body by
cleaning the blood of
harmful substances
that may have been
accidentally absorbed
by the small intestine.

liver

Supporting Cast

While most digestion occurs in the small intestine, many of the enzymes that aid digestion are made in the pancreas. The pancreas releases pancreatic juices, which contain hundreds of different enzymes. Each of these breaks down a specific nutrient into its basic building blocks. Pancreatic juices also help neutralize the acids from the stomach.

The gallbladder is a small, muscular sac that sits right underneath the liver. Its job is to store a special fluid called bile, which is a green liquid made in the liver. Bile contains special salts that help digest fats. When you eat a fatty meal, the gallbladder releases a small amount of bile into the small intestine to help dissolve and break down the fat.

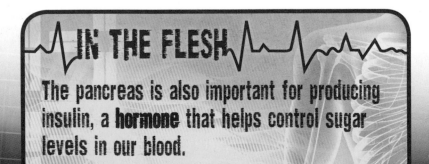

IN THE FLESH

The pancreas is also important for producing insulin, a **hormone** that helps control sugar levels in our blood.

When the stomach releases its contents into the small intestine, the gallbladder and pancreas are ready to help break down the nutrients.

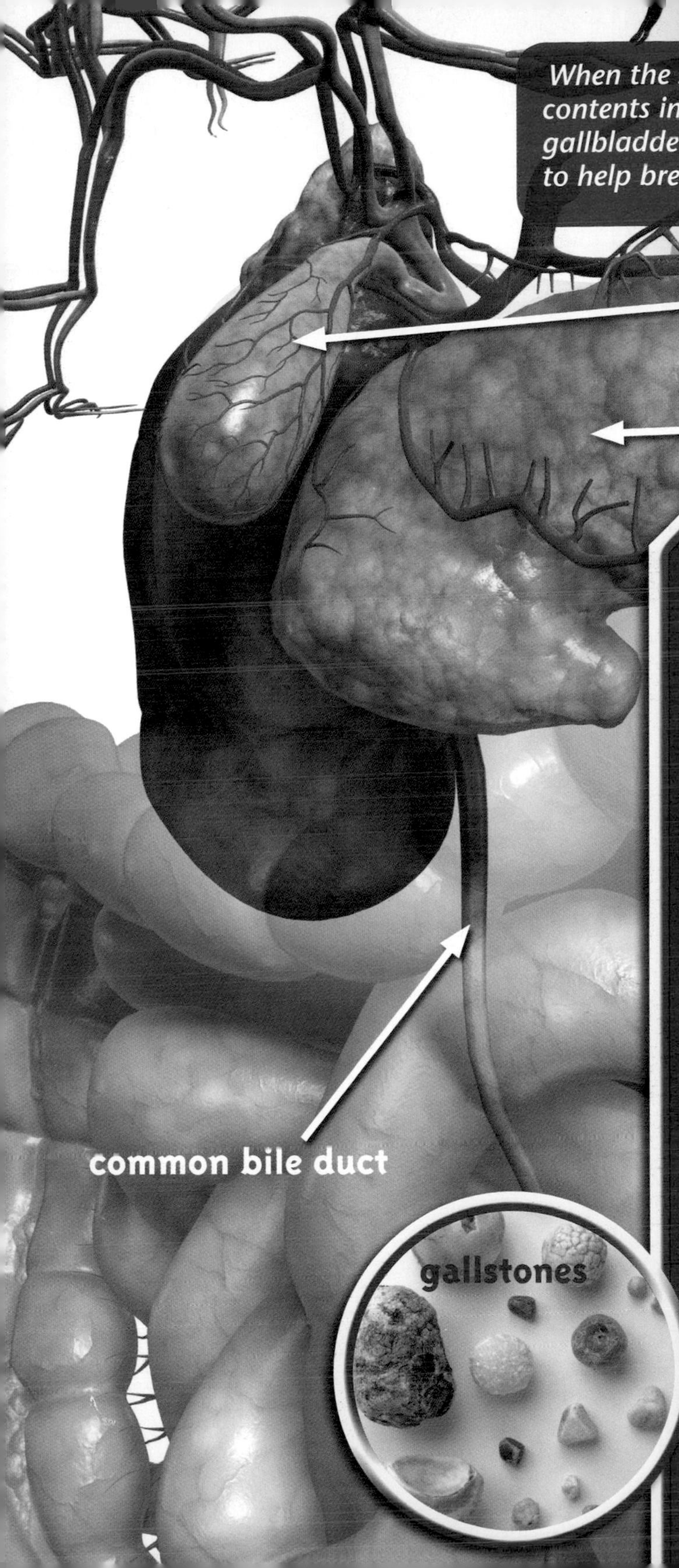

gallbladder

pancreas

The bile salts in the gallbladder usually stay dissolved in the bile, but sometimes they crystallize to form a hard material called a gallstone. When the gallbladder squeezes to release bile, it presses against the gallstone, causing pain. Eating meals that are low in fat can help prevent the pain. However, sometimes surgery is necessary to remove the stone.

common bile duct

gallstones

Completing Digestion

Most of our food's nutrients are digested and absorbed in the small intestine. The main job of the colon—the longest section of the large intestine—is to absorb water and minerals. About 4 pints (1.9 l) of watery material enter the colon daily, and about 3.6 pints (1.7 l) of water are absorbed into the blood. What's left is called feces, which is undigested food, fiber, and bacteria.

Feces travel though the colon the same way food travels down the esophagus and through the small intestine—by peristalsis. Normally, feces travel though the colon slowly, allowing the body time to absorb water. When we eat a meal, however, our brain signals the colon to speed up the transfer of feces to the rectum.

IN THE FLESH

When bacteria break down bile, it turns from green to brown, which makes feces brown as well.

BACTERIA IN THE COLON

Did you know there are more bacteria in your colon than there are cells in your body? These bacteria eat undigested food in your colon and are mostly beneficial. They help crowd out disease-causing bacteria that can make you sick. Some make vitamin K that your body can use. Human feces are about one-half undigested food and one-half living and dead bacteria!

The large intestine is twice as wide as the small intestine, but it's only 5 feet (1.5 m) long.

End of the Line

After water is absorbed from the undigested food waste, the colon pushes the remaining materials—feces—into the rectum. The rectum acts as a storage area until there's an appropriate time to eliminate the feces. This is a process known as defecation, or having a bowel movement.

Defecation is passage of the feces through the anus, which is the opening between the rectum and the outside world. Defecation is controlled by muscular rings known as sphincters. When we relax the sphincters, it allows the feces to pass from the body. You may find yourself holding your breath and pushing with your stomach. This increases pressure in the abdomen and helps push the feces out of the body.

IN THE FLESH

Together, the small intestine and large intestine are known as the bowel. This is where the phrase "bowel movement" comes from.

Half of feces is made of bacteria, some of which may make you or others sick. That's why it's important to wash your hands after going to the bathroom.

WHAT IS CONSTIPATION?

When we don't have a bowel movement as often as we normally do, the feces stay in the large intestine longer, and more water is absorbed. This makes the feces harder than normal and can make defecation more painful. This is called constipation. Everyone experiences constipation at some point, but it can be prevented by drinking plenty of water, eating plenty of vegetables, and staying active. Exercise can make feces travel through the colon faster.

Diseases and Disorders

By eating food and drinking water, we risk letting harmful bacteria into our bodies. The acid in our stomach helps kill most bacteria. However, some bacteria are very hardy and can give us food poisoning, which can cause vomiting ("throwing up") and stomach pain. These bacteria can live in undercooked meat, spoiled dairy products, and unwashed vegetables.

People can also get sick when they drink water that contains germs, such as the bacterium that causes the disease cholera. These germs stop the absorption of water in the colon, resulting in feces mixed with large amounts of water, or diarrhea. This can cause the body to lose a lot of water, which is harmful for important organs such as the kidneys and the brain.

IN THE FLESH

Washing and cooking food properly and making sure it is stored in the refrigerator afterwards are two ways to help prevent food poisoning.

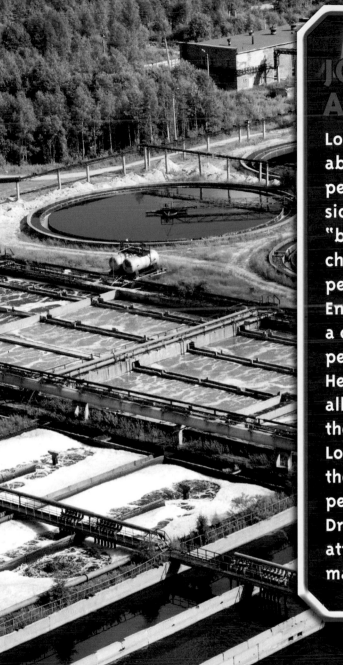

JOHN SNOW AND CHOLERA

Long before we knew about germs, many people thought we got sick from breathing "bad air." In 1854, cholera sickened many people in London, England. John Snow, a doctor, talked to the people who were sick. He discovered they all drank water from the same well. When London officials closed the well, far fewer people became sick. Dr. Snow's curiosity and attention to detail saved many people's lives.

Water treatment plants, such as the one pictured above, help keep our water supply clean and free from harmful, disease-causing bacteria.

A condition called appendicitis can cause great abdominal pain. Appendicitis is an **infection** of a small body part called the appendix, which is located where the small intestine meets the colon. It's a pouch about the size of your pinky finger. On very rare occasions, this pouch can get blocked by feces and bacteria. The bacteria continue to grow in the appendix. Since the opening to the pouch is blocked, the appendix begins to stretch, much like a balloon. This causes very severe pain in the abdomen.

If the appendix continues to stretch, it will eventually rupture, or burst. This will spread bacteria throughout the body, making the patient very sick very quickly. Surgeons must remove the infected appendix to stop the infection.

IN THE FLESH

Doctors don't know why we have an appendix. Removing the appendix has no effect on our health—except eliminating appendicitis!

Doctors must carefully examine all patients who experience abdominal pain to make sure they don't have appendicitis.

CT scan

IDENTIFYING ABDOMINAL PAIN

There are many causes of abdominal pain, and most don't need surgery. Hospitals have special machines that use a method called computed tomography, or CT, to scan the body for problems. These machines take hundreds of X-rays very quickly and put them together on a computer, which allows doctors to see inside the abdomen. Many doctors use **ultrasound** machines to see images of a patient's abdomen right at the bedside.

Sometimes the problems we have with our digestive systems are due to the foods we eat. Lactose is a type of carbohydrate found in diary products. For most people, lactose is broken down by enzymes found in the small intestine. However, one out of every six Americans is lactose **intolerant**. That means they can't digest lactose. This can result in abdominal pain, cramping, **nausea**, and diarrhea.

Gluten is a protein found in many types of flours, including wheat and rye. With celiac disease, the immune system thinks gluten is a germ and tries to attack the protein. Unfortunately, the immune system does a lot of damage to the digestive system during these attacks, which can cause abdominal pain, diarrhea, and bloating. These attacks can be prevented by avoiding foods that contain gluten.

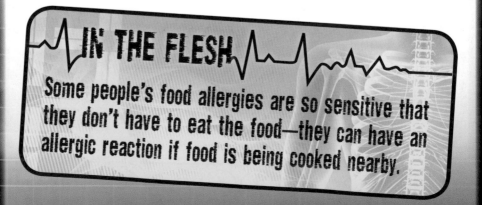

IN THE FLESH

Some people's food allergies are so sensitive that they don't have to eat the food—they can have an allergic reaction if food is being cooked nearby.

FOOD ALLERGIES

Some people experience very serious allergic reactions when they eat certain foods, such as peanuts or strawberries. The immune system thinks the food is a germ, so it releases chemicals to help fight the "infection." These chemicals can do incredible damage to the body. They can cause swelling around the windpipe, making it difficult for the person to breathe. People with food allergies must avoid even the tiniest piece of the food they are allergic to.

Fiber is an extremely important part of our diet, even though it doesn't supply any vitamins or minerals. Rather, fiber remains undigested as it travels though the digestive system. It provides the small and large intestines something to push against during peristalsis. Without fiber in the colon, peristalsis slows down and can even stop. The longer the feces stay in the colon, the more water is absorbed, and the harder the feces become. This can make defecation painful or difficult, resulting in constipation.

Scientists also believe a diet rich in fiber helps prevent diseases, such as **diabetes** and heart disease. Fiber can be found in most foods that come from plants, including vegetables, fruits, and whole wheat.

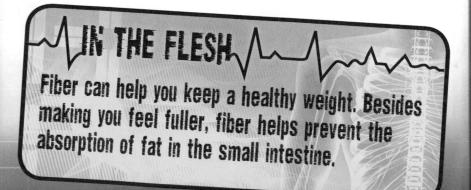

IN THE FLESH

Fiber can help you keep a healthy weight. Besides making you feel fuller, fiber helps prevent the absorption of fat in the small intestine.

Taking care of your digestive system begins with the part you see every day—your teeth!

WHAT'S ON YOUR PLATE?

In June 2011, the United States Department of Agriculture (USDA) did away with the old "food pyramid," replacing it with a simpler symbol of healthy nutrition. MyPlate shows the proportions of food groups that make up a balanced meal. Fruits and vegetables take up half a meal. Grains, half of which should be whole grains, take up a quarter of the plate. Proteins and dairy are also important, but they make up the smallest portions.

Fruits

Grains

Dairy

Vegetables

Protein

Choose**MyPlate**.gov

You can help maintain good digestive health by eating a wide variety of foods. Packaged and junk foods may taste good, but they're loaded with fat and sugar. Without other nutrients—such as protein and vitamins—to balance this, the excess fat is stored throughout the body. This can lead to a condition called obesity, which means weighing far more than you should for your height. It can also cause future medical problems, including diabetes, heart disease, **strokes**, and **cancers**.

As you can see from the chart, most vitamins and minerals come from fresh fruits and vegetables. Packaged food and junk food contain very small amounts of vitamins and minerals. Taking good care of your body begins by carefully choosing what you put inside it.

FACTS ABOUT
Vitamins and Minerals

		Where do we find it?
vitamins	A	carrots, leafy vegetables, butter, fish oil
	B_1, B_2, B_3, B_6, B_{12}	whole grains, nuts, many vegetables (B_{12}: fish, meat, dairy, chicken, eggs)
	C	citrus fruits (lemons, oranges), tomatoes
	D	fish, fortified milk, yogurt, eggs
	E	vegetables, meats, nuts
	K	leafy vegetables (lettuce, spinach, kale)
minerals	calcium	dairy products, leafy vegetables, grains
	iron	meat, nuts, eggs, leafy vegetables, beans, fish
	potassium	bananas, beans, nuts, fish
	sodium	meats, vegetables, breads
	zinc	fish, beans, eggs, meats, nuts

Glossary

bacteria: tiny creatures that can only be seen with a microscope

cancer: a disease caused by the uncontrolled growth of cells in the body

diabetes: a disorder that causes the body to produce excess urine and causes high levels of sugar in the blood

dissolve: to be absorbed in a liquid

enzyme: a protein made in the body that helps chemical reactions occur

hormone: a chemical made in the body that tells another part of the body how to function

hydrated: having a healthy amount of water in the body

immune system: the parts of the body that fight germs and keep it healthy

infection: the spread of germs inside the body, causing illness

intolerant: not able to eat a certain food or ingredient without getting sick

nausea: an unsettled feeling in the stomach

neutralize: to make something ineffective and remove its ability to cause harm

starch: a carbohydrate made by and stored in plants

stroke: a sudden blockage or break of a blood vessel in the brain

ultrasound: a method for seeing internal body parts using sound waves that people can't hear

For More Information

BOOKS

Macaulay, David. *The Way We Work: Getting to Know the Amazing Human Body*. Boston, MA: Houghton Mifflin, 2008.

Taylor-Butler, Christine. *The Digestive System*. New York, NY: Children's Press, 2008.

Walker, Richard. *Encyclopedia of the Human Body*. New York, NY: DK Publishing, 2002.

WEBSITES

How the Digestive System Works
health.howstuffworks.com/human-body/systems/digestive/digestive-system.htm
Learn about the digestive system by following what happens to a ham and cheese sandwich once it enters your mouth.

MyPlate
www.choosemyplate.gov
Visit the USDA's site to learn more about MyPlate as well as the healthy foods you can put on your plate during meals!

Your Digestive System
kidshealth.org/kid/htbw/digestive_system.html
This website is full of interactive and informative videos to help make learning about the digestive system fun.

Index